DRUGS AND MAN

Drugs and Man

JOHN GABRIEL NAVARRA

ILLUSTRATED BY TOBY NAVARRA

DOUBLEDAY & CO., INC.

GARDEN CITY, N.Y.

ISBN: 0-385-07956-7 Trade
0-385-00413-3 Prebound
Library of Congress Catalog Card Number 72-87474

Printed in the United States of America
9 8 7 6 5 4 3 2

PREFACE

The attention of almost everyone in the United States is focused on drug use. Too often, however, the focus is only on the so-called *harmful drugs*. But beneficial drugs can be abused, too! We must come to know the role that drugs can play in preserving life. And we must learn how to handle them so that drug abuse does not tear at the quality of our life.

I have tried to make the best facts available for your study in the pages that follow. Information that is acted on makes people free. I believe that you are intelligent. And I also believe that you are capable of making good decisions about your own conduct when you have good information.

Drug abuse is a complex problem. As many as twelve million people in the United States are using drugs in improper ways. The majority of the drug abusers are between the ages of nine and twenty-five. No one is sure how to solve the problem. Maybe you can help!

JOHN GABRIEL NAVARRA

Farmingdale, N.J.

To my grandchildren, Yolanda and John III,
that they may understand.

CONTENTS

BENEFICIAL DRUGS

The word *drug* has taken on many meanings in today's world. Ordinarily we think of a drug as a substance used to cure a disease. When a chemical is used to promote health or well-being, we say it is a beneficial drug.

Pneumonia is a disease of the lungs. In the 1930s one of every four people who got pneumonia died of the disease. Toward the end of the 1940s a chemical called *penicillin* was used to treat the disease. Fewer than one of every one hundred people who got pneumonia died when penicillin was used. There is no doubt that penicillin is a beneficial drug.

Physicians and Pharmacists

A physician—commonly called a *doctor*—uses many special instruments to discover why a person is ill. Discovering the cause of an illness is important. Healing takes place only after the cause is removed. The human body repairs itself and starts functioning as it should, once the cause of the illness is removed.

One way a physician may remove the cause of a disease from a person's body is to use a drug. A doctor will choose to use a drug only if that is the best treatment possible. If it is the best way, the physician will write a prescription.

A prescription is a written direction. You might say that a prescription is an order for a drug. On the order, the doctor places the name of his patient. He also writes a full description of the drug he has selected for his patient. The doctor is very careful to note the amount of the drug he wants his patient to have. In addition, he gives exact directions as to how often the patient is to use the drug.

When George Washington was President of the United States, most drugs were made from dried plants. In fact our word *drug* comes from the Dutch word *droog,* which means dry. A person who is skilled in preparing drugs for use is called a *pharmacist.*

A pharmacist studies a prescription when it is brought to him. He must be sure that he understands every part of the doctor's order. Then he prepares the drug. When

the preparation is complete, the pharmacist places a label on the container that holds the drug. On the label, the patient finds the directions he is to follow while using the drug.

Fighting Disease

Some diseases are caused by bacteria. Bacteria have the characteristics of both plants and animals. Organisms that cannot be identified as either plant or animal are classified as protists.

A bacterium consists of a single cell. It is too small to be seen by the unaided eye. For this reason scientists say that bacteria are microscopic.

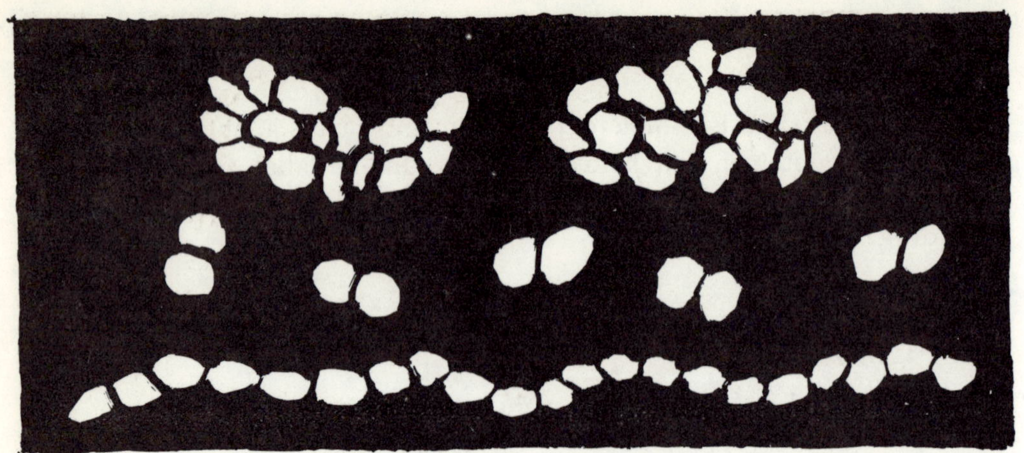

Some bacteria are round. They are called *cocci.* Round bacteria grow in pairs, in clusters, and sometimes in chains. The bacteria that cause pneumonia are round. They grow in pairs and are called *pneumococci.*

Bacteria that cause pimples and boils are round, too. When a doctor opens a pimple, he often finds that the bacteria are growing in grapelike clusters. The name given to these bacteria is *staphylococci.*

Another round type of bacteria is the *streptococcus.* These bacteria hang together like a string of beads. At times streptococci invade a person's throat. If they find good conditions, they begin to grow and multiply.

A bacterium, a single cell, multiplies by splitting into two. A single cell can grow and divide into two new bacteria in less than half an hour. This means that a single bacterium may divide over and over again. At the end of twenty-four hours there may be more than sixteen million bacteria in the place of the single bacterium.

Bacteria feed by digesting blood, muscle, and other tissue in the human body. As they feed, the bacteria give off poisonous waste products that upset the way the body functions. Some diseases caused by bacteria are: scarlet fever, whooping cough, diphtheria, pneumonia, tetanus, tuberculosis, and typhoid fever.

Diphtheria and tuberculosis are caused by bacteria that are shaped like rods. Rod-shaped bacteria are called

bacilli. Some bacteria are both rod-shaped and curved like a spiral. Such spirally curved bacteria are called *spirilla.*

Penicillin is a powerful bacteria killer that is produced by certain molds. This drug is very good as a destroyer of cocci, the round bacteria. Penicillin is used to fight many types of bacterial infections.

Remember, bacteria have some of the characteristics of plants. Plant cells have walls. Penicillin prevents developing bacteria from building walls. Penicillin prevents dividing bacteria from completing cell walls. As a result, the bacteria are destroyed.

Animal cells do not have walls. For this reason, penicillin does not disturb the functioning of a human cell. Penicillin is selective. When it is injected into muscle, penicillin seeks out and destroys bacteria without harming the human cells.

Relieving Pain

There are two types of drugs that ease pain: anesthetics and analgesics.

The first type, the anesthetics, ease pain by causing unconsciousness or by deadening nerve centers. Ether, for example, causes unconsciousness and a loss of feeling throughout the body. Novocain, an anesthetic used by dentists, causes a loss of feeling in a local area.

The second type of pain reliever, the analgesics, does not cause unconsciousness and does not deaden nerve centers. Aspirin and morphine are examples of analgesic-type drugs.

Almost everyone has had aspirin at one time or another. It is one of the most commonly used drugs. Aspirin is the common or trade name for acetylsalicylic acid. This chemical was first used in medicine more than eighty years ago.

Aspirin is a colorless, odorless powder. It does have a bitter taste, however. This drug is sold under many different trade names. It is purchased without a prescription.

Aspirin is most often used to relieve headache pain. It is also taken to reduce fever produced by a virus attack and other infections. People who suffer from pain produced by arthritis and rheumatism use aspirin, too.

Aspirin has been used for a long time. It is used because it works. Pain is relieved and fever is reduced. But there is a mystery about aspirin, too. No one is really sure how it works to ease pain and reduce fever.

In 1971, however, doctors began to peel away half the mystery about how aspirin works. Chemicals, prostaglandins, manufactured in the body, cause or induce fever. Aspirin, it was discovered, stops the manufacture of prostaglandins. By reducing these chemicals, aspirin reduces the fever. This, of course, is half the story. Aspirin eases pain, too. There is still half a mystery to solve.

Helping the Body Function

Sometimes the body does not work properly. Drugs can often be used to correct improper body function. Insulin and tolbutamide, for example, are two chemicals that are used when the body cannot handle sugar properly.

Diabetes is a disease that can occur when an organ of the body, the pancreas, does not function properly. The job of the pancreas is to produce insulin so that the body can use sugar properly. When the pancreas does not put out enough insulin, excess sugar is found in the blood and the urine. This condition affects blood circulation and makes the person an easy mark for other infections.

Most cases of diabetes cannot be cured. Physicians usually treat diabetes by prescribing injections of insulin and special diets. Sometimes a doctor selects tolbutamide in place of insulin. Tolbutamide is taken by mouth, and in some diabetics it drops the blood sugar to safe levels.

Preventing Disease

The best way to keep people healthy is to take steps to prevent them from getting a disease. You should, for example, have a thorough examination at least once a year. The yearly health check gives the physician an opportunity to study the way your body normally functions. He is then in a better position to identify a health problem before it gets out of hand.

At appropriate times the doctor will use drugs to help keep you free from disease. There are three main types of drugs he uses for this purpose: vaccines, serums, and germicides. Each is selected by the doctor at the right time to do a special job.

A vaccine usually contains dead bacteria or dead viruses. Sometimes a vaccine is made of live bacteria or live viruses. When live material is used, it is weakened. This prevents serious symptoms of the disease from developing before the body builds its defenses.

Most vaccines are injected into the body. Some, however, are given by mouth. A physician gives a vaccine to

a person before he is exposed to the disease. The material in the vaccine stimulates the body to develop defenses against the disease. Then, when a person is exposed to the disease, his body can fight off the viruses or bacteria that cause the disease.

Sometime before you entered school for the first time, you were given a vaccination against smallpox. You have also been given vaccinations against polio, diphtheria, and whooping cough. Each was given to prevent you from getting the disease if you are ever exposed.

Serums are different from vaccines. They do not contain bacteria or viruses—dead or alive. Serums contain materials called *antibodies,* which fight off the bacteria or viruses that cause certain diseases. These drugs are injected after a person has been exposed to a disease. Serums containing antibodies are called *antitoxic serums.*

Antitoxic serum is prepared in the following way: Bac-

teria that produce a particular disease are grown in a special fluid. The poisons, called *toxins,* given off by the bacteria are collected. The toxins are injected into a large animal. Antibodies develop in the animal's blood to fight off the poisons. Finally the blood is drained from the animal and the straw-colored fluid part of the blood, called *serum,* is separated. The antibodies are in the serum.

An antitoxic serum contains antibodies that fight poisons of a particular disease. Tetanus antitoxin is used to fight lockjaw. There are antitoxic serums that fight scarlet fever, pneumonia, dysentery, hepatitis, measles, and many other human diseases.

A germicide is a chemical that destroys bacteria and certain fungi. Chlorine placed in a swimming pool acts as a germicide. The silver-nitrate solution dropped into the eyes of a newborn infant is used to kill bacteria that might cause blindness. Both these chemicals used in the ways noted, prevent people from developing infections.

Tincture of iodine is one of the common drugs that many people use. It consists of the mineral iodine dissolved in alcohol. Tincture of iodine is a strong germicide.

When used on cuts and bruises, it prevents infection. Often, however, the alcohol evaporates and leaves the iodine so concentrated that it burns the skin and tissues. For this reason, most doctors prefer not to prescribe its use.

CAUTIOUS USE

Aspirin is a drug that is used by almost everyone. It is usually thought of as a safe drug. Some people, however, are sensitive and develop skin rashes when they take aspirin. And because it can be gotten without a prescription, some people take too much. A person who takes too much of a drug is said to have an overdose. An overdose of aspirin can produce some or all of the following effects: ringing in the ears, dizziness, dimness of vision, nausea, vomiting, and diarrhea.

You need to be careful with any drug. An overdose is dangerous. Always read the label on the container. Follow the directions printed on the label!

Sensitivity to Drugs

Sometimes a person is given a drug and he reacts to it by sneezing, itching, or developing a skin rash. A person who reacts in any of these ways is sensitive to the drug. These reactions are called *allergic reactions.*

Penicillin is a widely used drug. It helps the doctor fight and control many diseases. Some people, however, are allergic to penicillin. Allergic reactions to penicillin may show themselves as skin rashes, bleeding, or hives. These reactions can cause great discomfort.

Some people are so allergic to penicillin that it can

cause them to die. Physicians know about drug allergies. Before a prescription is written for a drug, the doctor must be sure the patient is not allergic to it.

Sulfa drugs are another group of chemicals that fight bacteria in the body. A sulfa drug does not attack bacteria directly. It works by stopping the manufacture of chemicals that certain bacteria need to grow. In other words, bacteria find themselves without food when sulfa goes to work. As a result, the bacteria die and the body begins to mend itself.

Sulfa drugs are used a lot because they work against many different kinds of bacteria. These drugs can be given by mouth or by injection. Sulfa can be applied directly to skin as an ointment or a powder. When it is applied directly, a person may become sensitive to it. Many people have allergic reactions to sulfa. It should be taken only when a physician has written a prescription for it.

At times, sulfa causes crystals to form in the kidneys and in the urine. A patient should always drink large

quantities of fluids when taking these drugs. Large amounts of water and fruit juice will prevent crystals from forming. A doctor is cautious. He will keep a close watch over you whenever you are taking a drug he has prescribed.

Side Effects

A doctor selects penicillin or some other antibiotic to fight a particular disease. But in addition to fighting the disease, the drug may cause some other things to happen inside the patient's body. The other things that happen are called *side effects.*

In a normal, healthy body there is a mixture of bacteria and yeasts in the bowel. Yeasts are very small fungi. When an antibiotic is taken by mouth, certain bacteria in the bowel are killed off. This allows other bacteria and fungi to multiply. If the fungus population gets too large, it causes an infection of its own. A fungus infection can cause trouble in the intestine. A fungus infection produced in this way is a side effect.

Chloromycetin is an antibiotic. It attacks a group of germs called *rickettsiae.* These germs are between bacteria and viruses in size. Typhus fever is one of the diseases caused by rickettsiae. Chloromycetin is a useful drug in fighting rickettsial diseases. A doctor prescribes this drug with caution, however. In some cases, chloromycetin causes damage to bone marrow and a person's ability to

produce blood. This is a very serious side effect when it occurs. Each time a doctor chooses a drug, he must weigh the benefits of using it against the side effects that may occur.

Sometimes a drug is used before the side effects are known. This happened in 1960. A drug called *thalidomide* was given to pregnant women in Europe. It was used as a sedative and as an anti-nausea medicine. By 1962 the side effects of this drug were being reported. Children were being born without arms and legs. Thalidomide caused the defects. It passed through the wombs of the women and changed the development of the unborn babies.

More than three thousand children were crippled by this drug. This did not happen in the United States, however, because Dr. Frances Kelsey was cautious. Dr. Kelsey, a government physician, felt that thalidomide had not been properly tested. As a result, our government did not release it for use.

The side effects produced by drugs can be very serious. Scientists are working on ways to predict what a person's reaction to a drug will be. Someday they may develop a simple test. Then a doctor will have a better way to select the drug he gives to a patient.

Magnesium is a chemical element that is needed by every cell in your body. It is very important for the proper functioning of brain cells. You must also have a good supply of magnesium in order to use the B vitamin called *pyridoxine.* A lack of magnesium or of pyridoxine can cause convulsions and tremors.

Antibiotics and drugs that remove water from the body destroy pyridoxine and decrease the amount of magnesium in the cells. If the level of either pyridoxine or magnesium falls too low, it may bring on a convulsion.

If the continued use of a drug decreases the amount of magnesium in the body, it can lead to a lot of difficulty. For example, when magnesium is in short supply, large amounts of calcium are lost in the urine. A loss of calcium can lead to poor bone development. It can also lead to rapid tooth decay.

A doctor must know the effect of every drug he prescribes. He knows the drugs that reduce your vitamin and mineral supply. The doctor will make sure that you are given additional vitamins and minerals during an illness.

Habit Forming

Analgesics are a group of drugs that ease pain. Aspirin is the common analgesic that everyone uses. Morphine is another analgesic. It is not used commonly. But it is used by physicians in certain cases.

Morphine was widely used for the first time during the Civil War between the states. The hypodermic needle had just been invented. So the doctors had a new tool to use.

They used the hypodermic needle to inject large amounts of morphine to ease the pain of wounded soldiers. The large doses the soldiers were given produced a hunger for the morphine in their bodies. The soldiers became morphine addicts.

An overdose of morphine is dangerous. The drug slows the movement of the lungs. If enough of the drug is taken, the lungs will stop functioning. This condition, of course, results in death.

Drugs called *barbiturates* are commonly prescribed today. These compounds are used to produce sleep. They are also given to calm, or relax, a nervous person. Barbiturates are used in the treatment of epilepsy, high blood pressure, and motion sickness. These drugs may also be given to a woman before the birth of a baby.

Ordinarily a patient develops an immunity to barbi-

turates after taking them for a few months. In order to get the same effect, the dose needs to be increased. Increasing the dose is dangerous. Barbiturates are habit forming.

Problems develop when the drug is suddenly stopped after a patient has been on medium-size doses for a long time. Such a person becomes agitated, sweats a lot, and cannot sleep. If he has been on large doses, he may go into a convulsion and die when the drug is stopped suddenly. The only safe way to withdraw a patient from barbiturates is to reduce the dose slowly.

AGENCIES THAT PROTECT

The Congress of the United States is the lawmaking branch of government. In 1938 Congress passed the federal Food, Drug, and Cosmetic Act. The act went into effect in 1940. Congress passed this act to protect the American people.

The act was written to make sure that new drugs are properly tested. If there is any question about a drug, it is not to be prescribed or put on sale. This act was used to hold thalidomide off the American market in 1960.

A number of government agencies see to it that this act of Congress is enforced. The Food and Drug Administration, the Federal Trade Commission, and the National Institutes of Health each plays a part in protecting us.

Food and Drug Administration: The FDA

Up until 1900 most people got their foods directly from farms and gardens. Then, at the turn of the century, many foods began to appear in cans and jars on grocery-store shelves. The processors began to add a lot of chemicals to the foods they placed in cans and jars. Some of these chemicals were used as preservatives, to keep foods from spoiling. Among the other chemicals added to foods were dyes. The dyes and preservatives were used to make the food appear fresh when in truth it was not.

In 1900 there was no restriction on the chemicals that could be added to foods. There were no restrictions on the sale of drugs, either. Both these situations were seen as a threat to the health of the American people. As a result, the first federal food and drugs act was passed by Congress in 1906. This act gave the federal government authority over interstate commerce in adulterated foods, drinks, and drugs.

The act of 1906 was a start. But it was a slow start. A separate agency that had the power to enter and inspect the plants of food processors and drug manufacturers was not created until 1928. This agency was called the *FDA* for the first time in 1931.

The Federal Food, Drug, and Cosmetic Act of 1938 gave the FDA new powers: Drugs had to be properly tested and properly labeled for the first time as a result of this act. But—strange as it may seem—a drug company still did not need to prove that a drug was effective in treating a disease. This was changed in 1962, however. Congress passed the Drug Amendments Act in 1962. By this action, Congress required a company to prove that a drug was effective as well as safe. Armed with this power, the FDA began to take a new look at drugs that were in use.

Cyclamates are a class of artificial sweeteners known chemically as *cyclohexyl sulfamates.* These chemicals were

first used as sweeteners in low-calorie foods in 1943. Although these sweeteners had been used for more than twenty-five years, FDA scientists began testing them again in the late 1960s.

In 1969 scientists reported that cyclamates produced bladder cancer in rats. They also found that these chemicals caused damage to threadlike strands, called *chromosomes,* inside the animals' cells. Chromosomes dictate an animal's characteristics and are, therefore, very important.

The FDA moved swiftly. Diet drinks containing cyclamates were removed from grocery-store shelves by January 1, 1970. Food processors were ordered to remove cyclamates from jams, jellies, desserts, and ice cream. It also became illegal to put cyclamates in canned fruits and vegetables, fruit and vegetable juices, concentrates for lemonade, iced-tea mixes, and certain groups of drugs.

When cyclamates were banned, in 1970, food processors turned to another artificial sweetener, called *saccharin.* Saccharin is not new. It has been used for more than eighty years by people who must avoid sugar. Saccharin is an organic compound containing sulfur. It is seven hundred times as sweet as natural cane sugar.

Recently, scientists at the Wisconsin Alumni Research Foundation fed twenty rats on a diet containing 5 percent

of saccharin. Three of the rats showed signs of having bladder tumors after a period of two years. Seven other research groups around the world are studying saccharin's effects on rats.

Even though all the evidence on saccharin is not in, the FDA acted. Saccharin was removed from the FDA's GRAS list in February 1972. GRAS stands for *generally recognized as safe*. In addition, FDA scientists set a limit on how much saccharin a person should use. And manufacturers have been told not to increase the amount of saccharin they use in their products.

In 1971 the FDA issued warnings against the use of the disinfectant hexachlorophene. This chemical is a good germicide. It attacks and destroys many bacteria, including staphylococcus. Unfortunately it also attacks the white matter of the brain if it is introduced into the body in large quantities.

The harmful effects of hexachlorophene were reported by scientists in 1971. They found that this chemical is

absorbed through the skin. Once it works its way through the skin, it moves into the blood stream. Then it flows with the blood into the brain, where it does its damage.

Hexachlorophene was introduced in the 1950s. It became a very popular germicide. This disinfectant was used in many skin cleaners, lotions, mouthwashes, deodorants, and soaps. It was also used in hospital nurseries to bathe the babies to keep them free of staphylococcus infections.

It is very important to have every chemical checked out long before it is put into use. Finding out about harmful effects twenty years after a drug has been put on the market is frightening.

National Institutes of Health: NIH

There are nine institutes that make up the NIH. The National Cancer Institute is probably the most famous of the nine. Each of the institutes carries out scientific studies on a major disease. The scientists at the National

Heart Institute, for example, devote their time to learning all about diseases of the heart.

The NIH, however, plays an important part in regulating certain drugs. Through its Division of Biologics Standards, the NIH is responsible for serums and vaccines. It controls the strength and purity of all serums and vaccines used in the United States.

World Health Organization: WHO

The WHO was established in 1948. It is a special agency of the United Nations. One of the activities of WHO is concerned with the control of epidemic diseases throughout the world. Another of its activities is directed toward setting up standards for drugs. It is important to have drug products of uniform strength and quality throughout the world.

Federal Trade Commission: FTC

The FTC is a United States Government agency. It was created in 1914. The commission consists of five members. They are appointed by the President of the United States. In making the appointments, the President seeks the advice and consent of the Senate. Each member of the commission serves for a seven-year term.

The commission has the power to investigate corporations and other business concerns. Its investigations are made to keep business competition free and fair. The FTC can report its findings to the Congress, the President, or the public. The commission has the power to issue a complaint against any company that is using unfair methods.

Today there is a great demand for consumer protection. This is especially true in the case of misleading advertising of products whose use might affect a person's health. Congress has stated that it will not allow false advertising of food, drugs, and cosmetics. The FTC has the responsibility for filing criminal charges against offenders.

There is a lot of advertising over radio and television, in newspapers, and in magazines today. The FTC has a special division that checks on all forms of advertising. Medical experts in this division check on the advertising of drugs. The FTC takes action against drug manufacturers that advertise falsely.

The Bureau of Customs

The bureau collects all duties, taxes, and fees that are due on goods imported into the United States. In recent years, one of the most important tasks of the customs

agent has been to enforce laws against smuggling. Great quantities of narcotic drugs are being brought illegally into our country.

Heroin and cocaine are two of the narcotic drugs being smuggled into the United States. These drugs are referred to as "hard" drugs.

A lot of the heroin is sent to France first. It is processed there and then sent by ship to Canada or South America. Smugglers find many ways to carry heroin across our borders.

Cocaine is produced in South America. We have a long border area that is difficult to patrol. The customs agents must stay alert to stop the flow of hard drugs into the United States.

OVER THE COUNTER

Each morning, the sun rises and millions of Americans rise with it. Some begin their day by reaching for a cigarette. Some prefer to start the day with a hot cup of coffee. And then there are some truly unfortunate people who feel they must begin with a drink of whiskey.

Each time a person reaches for a cigarette, coffee, or whiskey, he is reaching for a drug. These drugs are readily available. You don't need a prescription. They are found in the food market and in almost every restaurant.

There is no limit to the amount of these drugs that you can take. You make the choice. In order to make an intelligent choice, you need information. In the pages that follow, you will find some information concerning how these drugs affect people.

Tobacco

The Surgeon General is the physician in charge of the United States Public Health Service. On January 11, 1964, the Surgeon General of the United States released a report on smoking and health. The report was based on more than eight thousand studies made by scientists throughout the world.

Three conclusions from this report on the relationship of smoking to health are important:

Conclusion 1. Cigarette smoking is causally related to lung cancer in men. The death rate from lung cancer is almost eleven times greater for men who smoke than for men who do not smoke. The conclusion concerning women points in the same direction.

Conclusion 2. The death rate from bronchitis and emphysema of the lungs is more than six times greater for smokers than for non-smokers.

Conclusion 3. The death rate from heart disease is almost twice as great for men who smoke as for non-smoking men.

Ten highly qualified scientists spent fourteen months putting together this report. It is their conclusion that cigarette smoking is a hazard to health.

The Federal Trade Commission, you will recall, has been given some broad powers by Congress. The FTC studied the Surgeon General's report and then decided to act. On June 24, 1964, the FTC ordered that all cigarette

packages must carry warnings that smoking endangers health and can cause cancer. The same FTC order required warnings in other forms of cigarette advertising, too.

An interesting study was reported by Dr. Harry Daniell in 1971. He studied the facial wrinkles of smokers and non-smokers. Dr. Daniell observed and measured the wrinkles at the "crow's-foot" area, at the outer corner of each eye. In every age group, he found that the most heavily wrinkled people were the smokers. Dr. Daniell concluded from his study that smoking can result in the early onset of deep facial wrinkles.

Nicotine in cigarette smoke causes the small blood vessels in the skin to contract. Dr. Daniell thinks that over a period of time this causes skin tissue to deteriorate and wrinkles to develop.

The fact that nicotine causes small blood vessels to contract produces another effect, too. The facial skin color of smokers is more likely to be yellow or grayish than pink. The blood supply to cells in the face is cut when the nicotine causes the vessels to contract.

The action of nicotine on blood vessels also explains why smokers almost never blush. When a person blushes, it means that a good supply of blood is flowing close to the surface of his skin. This happens when emotions cause the small blood vessels near the skin surface to enlarge, or dilate. The action of nicotine, on the other hand, keeps the blood vessels contracted and prevents blushing.

What does this all mean? It means that cigarette smok-

ing affects the flow of blood through the body. Blood carries nourishment to each and every cell in the body. When cells are not nourished properly, problems develop.

Another recent study reports that a large number of heavy cigarette smokers cannot hear low-pitched sounds. Some doctors believe that the hearing loss is the result of smoke damage to the eustachian tube and the cochlea. The eustachian tube connects the nose and throat with the middle ear. The cochlea is a part of the inner ear. It is possible that the damage occurs because nicotine decreases the flow of blood to the hearing mechanism. Over a long period of time, this loss of nourishment may cause the hearing loss.

We have known for a long time that vitamin C is essential to health. It is necessary to normal bone and tissue growth. We have also known that white blood cells protect the human body from infection. Recent evidence

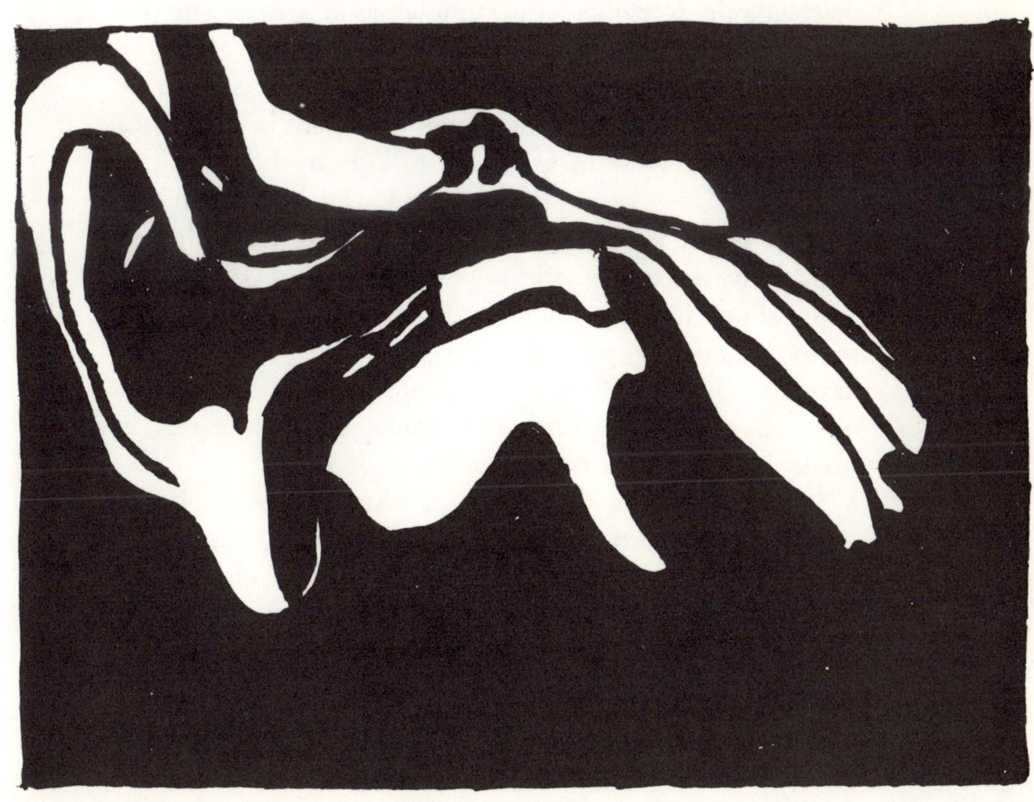

suggests that vitamin C plays a role in this process of protection.

The discovery that vitamin C may help fight infections was made at the Bowman Gray School of Medicine in Winston-Salem, North Carolina. Physicians at the school were studying the blood of patients whose white cells did not repel infection. They found that the defense cycle was improved when vitamin C was added. It is believed that vitamin C works as a stimulator, or trigger, in the defense cycle.

Smoking destroys vitamin C. When a foreign substance such as nicotine reaches the blood, it is more or less toxic, or poisonous. Vitamin C moves to rid the body of the poison. And, as a result, the vitamin C is destroyed. When the vitamin C level is lowered by smoking, the defenses of the body are weakened.

A sad fact has recently been discovered. You don't have to do the smoking yourself to be affected by it. Scientists have found that children who live in smoky homes have reduced physical health. The home, in such cases, is smoky because both parents smoke.

Trouble can develop for a non-smoker when he is constantly exposed to cigarette smoke. For example, a physician noted that a child's severe asthma cleared up when his mother stopped smoking. The asthma returned when the mother started smoking again.

Cadmium, a toxic metal, is found in tobacco smoke. This metal is a health hazard to smokers and non-smokers. Scientists have found that smoke drifting from the burning end of a cigarette carries most of the cadmium with it. This may be harmful to anyone reached by the smoke. Large doses of cadmium can cause acute poisoning.

Alcohol

Alcohol increases the need for the B vitamins in the human body. These vitamins are needed to use the alcohol in the body. It has been known for a long time that people who drink large quantities of alcohol develop vitamin B deficiencies.

Thiamine is one of the B vitamins. Alcohol reduces the level of this vitamin in the body. A deficiency in this vitamin affects the heart. It produces a type of heart-muscle weakness.

You have already read about the relationship between magnesium and pyridoxine, one of the B vitamins. Even small amounts of alcohol cause a loss of magnesium in the body. The magnesium passes out of the body through the urine. A heavy drinker who does not add magnesium to his diet is asking for a heart attack and other problems.

Some people crave alcohol. They become addicted to it. The cause of alcohol addiction may be the formation of morphine-like drugs within the body. This may seem strange, because alcohol and morphine are quite different chemically. But the action that each of these drugs has on the brain is produced by very similar substances.

In recent years alcohol has been found to be the culprit in the increasing number of deaths due to choking. Death in these cases results when a piece of food becomes caught in the larynx, at the top of the windpipe. In 88 per cent of such deaths in Broward County, Florida, the person was under the influence of alcohol.

Alcohol acts as an anesthetic. It causes a certain loss of sensation. As a result, the eater is less aware of the size of the piece of food in his mouth. This drug causes a loss of judgment, too. A person who is drinking and eating

becomes less able to decide when food is ready to be swallowed. As the alcohol content of the blood increases, there is some paralysis of motor functions. Swallowing and walking are both motor functions.

A person is in danger when his sensations, judgment, and motor functions are not operating properly. You don't have to be driving a car to fear for your life. Death sits down at a dinner table, too, when a person has had too much alcohol.

Caffeine

Caffeine is found naturally in coffee. It is added to cola drinks to give them pep. Caffeine is a stimulant and it is a drug.

Some people find it difficult to go to sleep after they

have had a drink with caffeine in it. Other people get jittery and nervous when they have had too much coffee. Some coffee is processed to take the caffeine out of it. It is called *decaffeinated coffee.*

Some recent studies have shown that damage to chromosomes can be caused by caffeine. Chromosomes, remember, dictate a person's characteristics. Two Utah scientists say that chromosome breakage may cause the body to degenerate, or grow older. If this is the case, caffeine may speed aging.

Under normal conditions, the body can repair some

chromosome damage. Aging occurs when the breakage gets ahead of the body's ability to make repairs. Heavy coffee drinkers may be tipping the balance so the body cannot keep up with the repair work.

Caffeine stimulates the heart. This causes an increased flow of blood to move through the kidneys. And, as a result, more B vitamins are lost in the urine.

A heavy coffee drinker usually has very low levels of B vitamins in his body. This is true even when his diet is excellent. It is difficult for the body to hold onto enough of the B vitamins when the intake of caffeine is high. Many heavy coffee drinkers suffer from vitamin B deficiencies.

SELLING BY PROPAGANDA

Newspapers, magazines, radio, and television are supported in our country by advertising. There are only a few television stations that get their operating money from some other source. Advertising plays a big part in our lives.

The goal of advertising is to sell a product. When the product is presented to the public in a proper and fair way, advertising serves a useful purpose. Part of a fair presentation, of course, means that it is based on facts.

Good advertising is meant to inspire the public with the desire to buy. Too often, however, advertising is not in the public interest. It is not based on fact. And it is misleading. When drugs are sold in this way, great harm can be done to the public health.

Each ad has its own appeal. Usually the appeal is made to one of the desires that prompt human behavior. Most people, for example, desire to be comfortable.

Examine the ad below. How does it appeal to a person's desire for comfort? Are there any statements that might be misleading?

Some advertising promises better quality or a superior product. Study the ad on this page. The appeal of a superor product is made on the basis of how fast the sleeping pill works. Nothing is said about how safe the drug is.

An ad often seeks to get a person's attention by an interesting picture or by asking a question. Both of these techniques are used in the ad on this page. Once the reader's attention is gotten, there is usually another message. In the ad below, an association is made between good friends and the best Bourbon.

When selling a product that competes with others, an advertiser tries to present *reasons why* his product should be bought. Study the ad on this page. It is a reason-why ad. But remember the warning: The Surgeon General has determined that cigarette smoking is dangerous to your health.

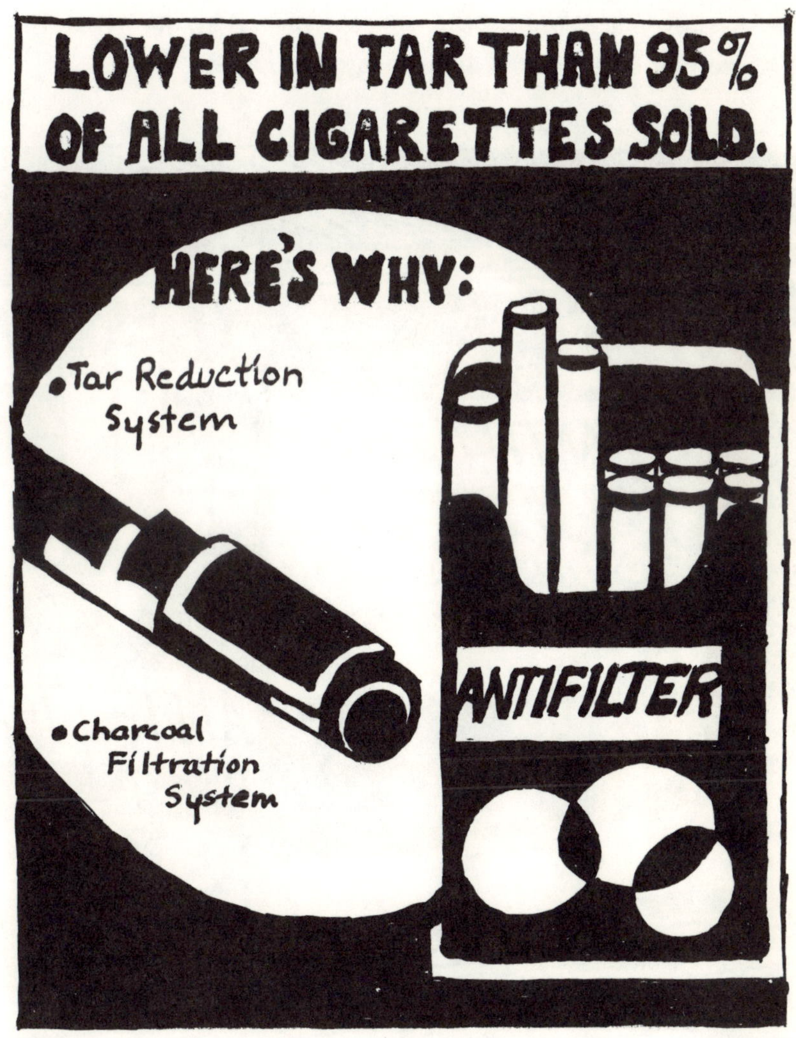

Suggestion advertising is used a lot. The suggestion comes from a picture. The picture usually shows the product being used in a setting that has some appeal or prestige.

The cigarettes are associated with an appealing setting. The people are involved in an enjoyable activity. A person looking at the ad is expected to associate the enjoyable activity with the cigarettes.

The bottled drink is in the hands of nurses. This is a hospital setting. We usually associate nurses with health. A person looking at the ad is expected to feel that the product is good if it is used by the nurses.

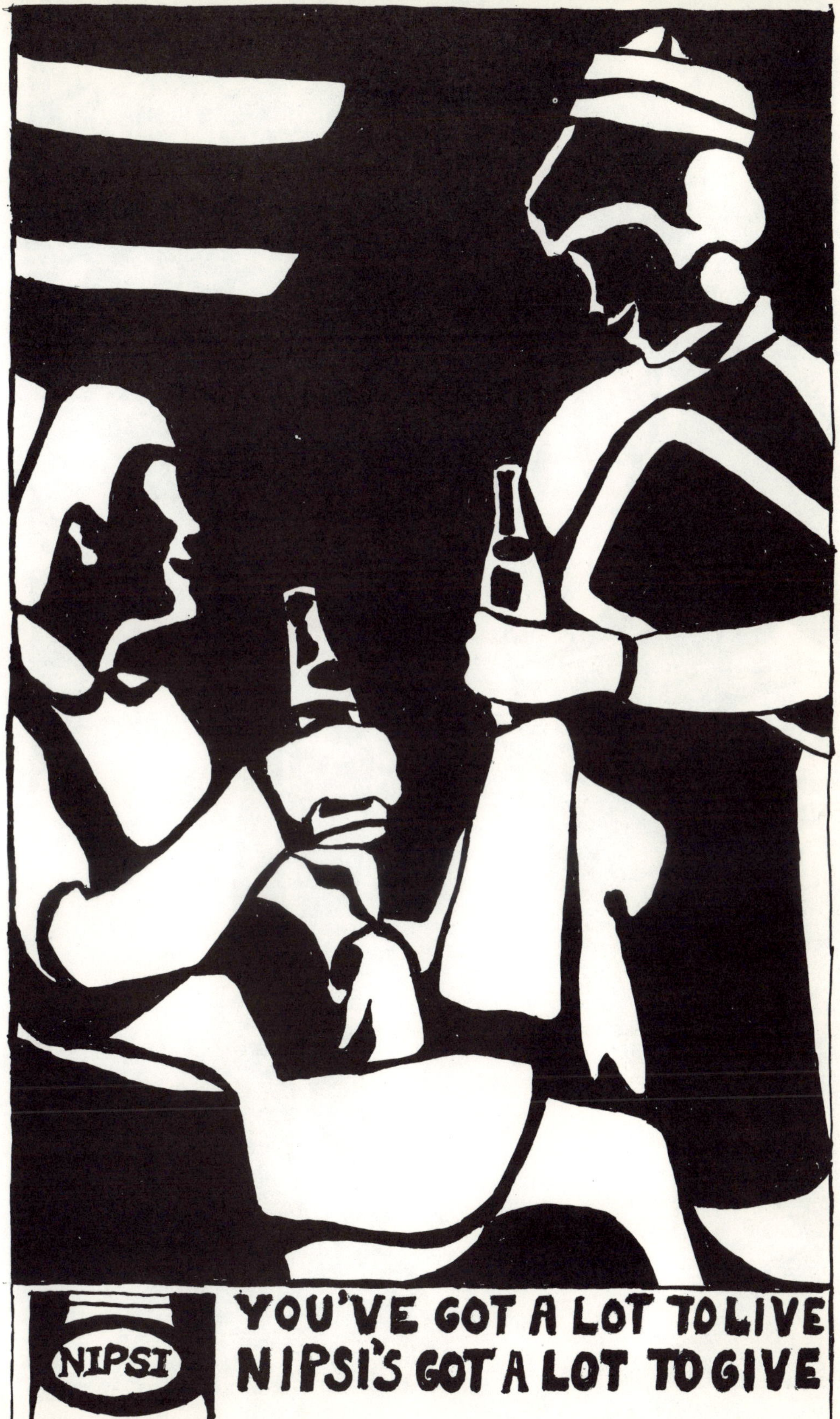
NIPSI
YOU'VE GOT A LOT TO LIVE
NIPSI'S GOT A LOT TO GIVE

HARMFUL DRUGS

You have read about the effects of a lot of drugs in this book. Most of these drugs have had an effect on the body. In this section of the book you are going to read about drugs that have an effect on the mind.

When a chemical has an effect on the mind, it is called a *mind-altering drug*. Most of the mind-altering drugs create a desire in the person to use them again and again. In many cases, the person develops a craving for the drug. We usually say that a person with a craving for a drug is addicted. Addiction means to be physically dependent upon a drug.

Marijuana

Marijuana is a drug that affects a person's control. It is obtained from the flowers and top leaves of the Indian hemp plant. This plant grows in most parts of the world.

Because it grows so widely, marijuana has been used by people since ancient times. In the Near and Middle East, it is known as *hashish.* Hashish is the dark-brown material that is collected from the tops of the Indian hemp plant. Hash, as it is sometimes called, is at least five times stronger than crude marijuana.

In the United States, marijuana is usually rolled into cigarettes and smoked. The cigarettes are called *joints.* This drug is also smoked in ordinary pipes and water pipes. Sometimes it is added to food and drink.

When marijuana is taken, it has an effect on the mind. The sense of hearing and the sense of seeing are functions of the brain. Both these senses become distorted. Thought becomes dreamlike, and the sense of time does not function well.

Marijuana produces some physical effects, too. The whites of the eyes become red. The heart begins to beat

more rapidly. And usually a cough develops, because the smoke irritates the lungs.

Most scientists say that marijuana does not lead to physical dependence. The effects of long-continued use, however, are not scientifically known.

Some scientists believe that the heavy use of marijuana may have an effect on the developing personality of a young person. This happens when the young person uses marijuana to avoid the normal difficulties of life. Facing and overcoming the small problems of life helps a person to grow up and develop his mind to the fullest.

Stimulants

Stimulants are drugs that make a person more alert. They also reduce hunger and give a person a feeling of well-being. A physician may prescribe these drugs when a person is on a diet. He may also give these drugs to a patient who is feeling depressed.

Some of the common stimulants are cocaine, amphetamine, and methamphetamine. Stimulants are also called *uppers* and *pep pills.* Methamphetamine is sometimes called *speed* or *crystal.*

Stimulants may be in the form of tablets or capsules. A tablet is taken by mouth. Speed and cocaine in the form of powder can be inhaled, or snorted, through the nose. These drugs can also be injected into veins. Whenever a drug is injected, its effects are stronger and are felt more rapidly.

Amphetamines increase the amount of a chemical, noradrenalin, at the nerve-cell connections in the brain. Large amounts of amphetamines may cause a person to become talkative, overactive, and irritable. In some cases, a person on speed becomes violent.

A person who is addicted to amphetamines finally becomes physically exhausted. He develops shakiness, itching, muscle pains, and tension. Larger doses must be taken each time to reach the "high." Liver damage may occur from the huge amounts of the drug that are taken. Brain damage is known to occur in animals that have been placed on large doses of these drugs.

Cocaine is a white, crystalline chemical obtained from the coca plant. This bush is found growing wild in Peru, Bolivia, and Chile. The coca bush is cultivated in many countries throughout the world.

The Indians of the Andes Mountains of South America have used this drug for centuries. They chew the coca leaves. Used in this way it produces a local anesthetic of the stomach. This allows them to withstand hunger and thirst. The stimulating effect of the drug increases their ability to work and walk in the high mountain areas.

In the United States, cocaine is known as *snow*. As a fine white powder, it is often sniffed and absorbed through the mucous membranes of the nose. This drug has a toxic action on the central nervous system. When first taken, it produces a stimulating effect. This is followed by a feeling of depression as the effect of the drug wears off. Addiction to cocaine can develop within a week or two of its first use.

Small doses of cocaine stimulate the cortex of the brain. Large doses stimulate the spinal cord. This is very dangerous and convulsions can result. If the whole nervous system becomes depressed as the effect of the drug wears off, the respiratory system may stop functioning. This, of course, results in death to the addict.

Sedatives

The barbiturates are the largest group of sedatives. When these drugs are taken in small doses, they reduce tension and anxiety. Sedatives are prescribed by physicians. These drugs are also used in sleeping pills.

Barbiturates are physically addicting. Other addicting sedatives are gluthethimide and chloral hydrate. In the United States, sedatives are called *sleepers, downers,* and *goof balls.*

A person who is nervous or cannot sleep may begin taking a sedative. The body builds up a tolerance to the drug. To get the same relaxing effect, the dose has to be increased. After a few weeks on large doses of a sedative, a person develops a strong desire to continue taking the drug.

Sometimes a person addicted to amphetamines begins using sedatives, too. Amphetamines, remember, make a person jittery. The addict then turns to the barbiturates to calm himself down. He really gets caught up in a vicious cycle of uppers and downers.

People who take large doses of sedatives can go into a coma. If a person has built a tolerance to large doses, he may stay awake but he will appear to be drunk. His speech will be slurred and his movements will not be co-ordinated. A person in this state will be confused. His judgment and his ability to see will not be good.

A combination of sleeping pills and alcohol is very dangerous. Even small doses of alcohol and sedatives can cause death when taken together.

Lysergic Acid Diethylamide: LSD

Ergot is a parasitic fungus. It attacks rye, wheat, and barley. Ergot is the source of a number of drugs. Lysergic acid comes from ergot. LSD is derived from lysergic acid.

LSD is a drug that can produce changes of sensation, thinking, and emotion. It also changes the way a person "sees" time and space.

When a person sees a misleading image, we call it an *illusion.* When the image is completely unreal and there is no basis in fact for it, we call it a *hallucination.* LSD causes people to have illusions and hallucinations. For this reason, LSD is called a *hallucinogen.*

LSD is one of a large number of drugs that produce illusions and hallucinations. Peyote and mescaline, which are obtained from the peyote cactus, belong to this group of drugs. Psilocybin—obtained from a Mexican mushroom —and the seeds of the common morning glory are hallucinogens, too.

A number of effects show up as soon as a person takes LSD. The pupils in his eyes begin to enlarge, or dilate. His face becomes flushed and red. His heart is affected and begins to beat faster. The body temperature of a person who has taken LSD rises. But even though his body temperature is up, the person feels chilly.

LSD users talk about "good trips" and "bad trips." They consider it to be a good trip when they see pleasant

images and get pleasant feelings. If the images are unpleasant and frightening, they consider it to be a bad trip. They talk about a bad trip as a "bummer." LSD users have been known to commit suicide.

Some scientists have reported that LSD can damage chromosomes. A lot of scientific work is being done on the effects of LSD.

Narcotics

Narcotics are drugs that relieve pain. This group of drugs includes opium, morphine, heroin, and codeine.

Opium is a narcotic made from the juice of poppies. Opium poppies grow to heights of three and four feet. These plants are cultivated in many parts of the world. Poppies from which opium is made legally are grown in Turkey, India, and Egypt.

A thick, milky juice flows throughout the opium poppy. Opium is produced from the juice of the unripened seed pod. Workers slit the green seed pod as soon as the petals

of the poppy flower fall. As the juice oozes out, it is collected and dried. The dried juice is brown, gummy, and sticky. Chemists refine the dried juice until it becomes a white powder.

Pure white opium powder has a distinct odor and a sharp, bitter taste. Physicians do not use pure opium powder. They use chemical compounds made from opium. Morphine, heroin, and codeine are made from opium.

Opium smoking is illegal in almost all parts of the world. But it is done nevertheless. Opium is prepared for smoking by boiling with water and then toasting it. Many people in India, Indonesia, and the Far East smoke opium. Opium produces physical and mental problems for those who become addicted to it.

The active ingredients of opium are chemicals called *alkaloids.* Morphine is the most important alkaloid of opium. It makes up about 10 per cent of the total alkaloids found in opium.

Morphine is a useful painkiller when used by a skilled physician. Severe pain often develops in a fatal illness. People dying of cancer can be given morphine to ease the pain.

The pleasant effects of morphine last from four to six hours. As the drug wears off, the skin begins to flush and itch due to the release of chemicals called *histamines.* This is often followed by giddiness and vomiting.

Many people in the United States are morphine addicts. Morphine addiction makes a person a physical and mental wreck. Many addicts die as a result of an overdose of the drug. An overdose of morphine slows the action of the lungs until they stop.

Heroin is a drug that is made from morphine. As a painkiller, it is from four to eight times more powerful than morphine. Originally heroin was developed as a substitute for morphine because morphine produced so much addiction. But experience has shown that heroin is even more dangerous than morphine. People become addicted to heroin more easily than morphine.

Heroin that is bought on the street is almost always diluted with milk, sugar, or other materials. As a result, the material is not sterile. A person injecting this material into his system can introduce infection into his body in addition to becoming an addict. Heroin addicts are exposed to many bacterial diseases, as well as hepatitis. They also develop skin abscesses, inflammation of the veins, and congestion of the lungs.

The heroin addict does not live to a ripe old age. His life expectancy is very low. Addiction also causes problems in the reproductive system of both male and female.

When a child is born of a woman who is a heroin addict,

the child may develop withdrawal symptoms. In other words, the child became an addict while being carried in his mother's womb.

Codeine is another of the alkaloids that is found in opium. It is a derivative of morphine. And it has the same properties as morphine. But codeine is much weaker. Codeine can be taken by mouth. Or it can also be injected into the body with a hypodermic needle.

Codeine is used in the preparation of cough syrups. A cough syrup that contains codeine should be taken only when it is prescribed by a physician. And it should not be taken over a long period of time.

Paregoric is a medicine that contains powdered opium. It acts as an intestinal sedative. It is used by physicians to treat diarrhea. Anyone who takes paregoric must be careful to follow the physician's directions.

PROBLEMS OF ADDICTION

At this point in your reading, you have looked over some information about drugs. You know something about the different kinds of drugs. You have learned that even the beneficial drugs can be abused and can have harmful effects.

All through this book I have tried to make you aware of the problems that develop when drugs are abused. I have tried to give you the facts—the best facts that scientists have at this time. I believe that you are intelligent and that you have drawn some conclusions of your own.

In the six pages that follow, I am going to summarize and draw some conclusions. Some are my own. Some are conclusions that scientists have made concerning what happens when a person becomes addicted. You may disagree. If you do, these pages may help you to take another look at your own conclusions.

Loss of Judgment

No one will dispute the fact that alcohol can cause drunkenness. When we say a person is drunk, we mean that he has a loss of judgment. In other words, he loses some of his ability to make decisions. He will not react quickly or correctly.

What many people fail to realize is that barbiturates and other drugs can produce some of the same effects. A person taking barbiturates will, at times, appear to be drunk. His vision will be blurred. His speech will be slurred. And his movements will not be co-ordinated.

A person who is drunk—whether from alcohol or another drug—is a menace when he is involved in some activities. A person who is drunk can step from a curb and be killed by an automobile. A drunk driver kills. He can kill himself and others.

The problem is that a drunk person is the last to know that he is drunk. Think about this: The loss of judgment caused by a drug can prevent a person from realizing that there is anything wrong with his co-ordination or the way he sees things.

Psychological Disturbance

Heavy use of LSD may cause problems with a person's memory. He will begin to forget things. Such a person may lose some of his ability to do abstract thinking. He may find that his attention span is affected, too, and he is not able to concentrate on anything for very long.

A person who has taken LSD may have "flashbacks." This means that he goes into an LSD trip even though it is days or months since the last dose. Stress, marijuana, or even a beneficial drug taken for good medical reasons can trigger the beginning of the trip. Flashbacks can be horrifying. A person who experiences a number of flashbacks becomes anxious. He begins to feel that he is going mad. Some people who have flashbacks commit suicide.

LSD is not the only drug that produces psychological problems. A person who is on narcotics also has these problems. He lives in constant fear that he will not be able to get the drug when he needs it. When a person is addicted, stopping the drug causes withdrawal sickness.

In the case of heroin, withdrawal sickness begins from twelve to sixteen hours after the last injection. At the onset of the sickness, the addict begins to yawn, shake, and sweat. His nose and eyes run and he vomits. His muscles begin to ache and jerk. This is where the expression "kicking the habit" comes from. The addict going through withdrawal also gets severe stomach pains and diarrhea. This may be followed by hallucinations that are truly terrifying.

There is a withdrawal sickness associated with most of the harmful drugs. For example, a person addicted to alcohol, barbiturates, or some other drugs may have a convulsion if the drug is suddenly withheld. Hallucinations and high fever are also commonly experienced by alcoholics during withdrawal.

Dangerous to Others and Himself

One of the main goals of the drug addict is to get more drugs. You might say he lives for drugs. Many addicts neglect all other obligations. An adult addict usually becomes an unreliable worker. If an addict has children, he will often tend to neglect them, too.

The addict needs money. He needs the money to get drugs. Sometimes the addict feels that the only way to get the money is to turn to crime. Many addicts are capable of using violence to get the money to support their drug habit.

We usually think of violence in terms of the injury that an addict inflicts on someone else. But there is another kind of violence we should think about—the violence an addict inflicts on himself when he takes a drug.

In 1971 a team of British doctors studied ten young men. These boys had smoked marijuana for three to eleven years. In addition, they used pep pills and LSD. Marijuana, however, was the basic drug they used. In each of the ten cases, the doctors reported that there was permanent brain damage. The technical name for the damage is *cerebral atrophy.* It means that brain tissue has shrunk.

When brain tissue shrinks, it can cause headaches and a loss of memory. It also changes a person's personality. A person with shrinking brain tissue does not think clearly and he begins to lose his desire to work.

When someone is struck on the head, we think of it as a violent act. Brain damage, of course, can be produced by a knock on the head. When brain damage results from taking drugs, it is just as violent an act, in my opinion. And the person does it to himself! Society tries to protect people from getting struck on the head. Does society have an obligation to protect someone from the blow that a drug can give to his brain?

TREATMENT

Many people believe that once a person is an addict he will always be an addict. This is not true. A lot of people have been able to "kick the habit." It isn't easy. But it can be done. Once a person frees himself, he can become a useful citizen again. Former drug addicts say that "it's like being reborn."

There are many different kinds of treatment procedures in use. Some treatment programs are run by the federal government. Others are run by state governments. There are a few very effective programs run by former addicts. If a person on drugs really wants help, he can find it!

Hospital Care

The first step in treating an addict is to reduce the amount of the drug he is taking. This is done slowly, under a physician's watchful eye. Each day, the addicted person is given a smaller dose than he was given the day before. Stopping a drug suddenly, remember, can cause withdrawal sickness.

Even after a person has been withdrawn from a drug completely, he needs help. The doctors prescribe a program of care that helps the ex-addict to become stronger both physically and mentally.

The United States Public Health Service operates two hospitals for drug addicts. One center is located at Lexing-

ton, Kentucky. There is another center at Fort Worth, Texas. In addition, there are about sixteen community centers in various sections of the country that are supported by the federal government.

The British System

Until 1968, heroin addicts in England were able to obtain the drug by prescription after registering with a physician. Under this procedure, the number of addicts grew rapidly. As a result of the great increase in addiction, the system was changed in 1968.

The new system used in England depends on centers where the addict receives treatment. However, in those cases where total withdrawal does not seem possible, the British still allow the person to have some of the drug by prescription.

Methadone

Methadone is a man-made narcotic. A person placed on methadone becomes addicted to it. Physicians, however, have found that methadone can be useful to block the mental effects of heroin for some addicts.

Methadone is used as a treatment for heroin addiction. The addict is given methadone by mouth as a substitute for heroin. But the treatment, remember, is not a cure. A person on methadone is still addicted. Instead of being addicted to heroin, he is now dependent on methadone.

There is an advantage in replacing heroin with methadone, however. The patient develops socially acceptable behavior when he is put on methadone. The methadone addict obeys the law, and he can work and is generally a useful member of society.

Narcotic Antagonists

When heroin is injected into the body, it moves to nerve cells and attaches itself to them. From its position on a nerve cell, the chemical we call *heroin* influences nerve-cell reactions.

A narcotic antagonist is a drug that occupies the same position on a nerve cell that heroin occupies. In other words, if an antagonist is released into the body, it can be used to hold heroin off a nerve cell. By holding heroin off, the antagonist prevents heroin from doing its dirty work on a nerve cell.

Cyclazocine is a narcotic antagonist. It is a safe agent that sits on a nerve cell and blocks heroin. If heroin is taken after cyclazocine, no effect is observed. The person does not experience the heroin high.

Scientists are searching for new and improved narcotic antagonists. Physicians are studying ways in which these chemicals can be used to fight drug addiction.

Encounter Programs

There are a number of programs that use the encounter method. Basically, the encounter is between an addict and a group of ex-addicts. The addict patient is made to face his problems and talk them through. The ex-addicts listen to him. They challenge him to be honest and face his problems.

One of the most successful programs of the encounter type is Synanon. This kind of treatment seems to work because ex-addicts are not taken in by an addict's stories and lies. Ex-addicts can help, because they have faced the same difficulties. They know a person can make it. But he must have the desire and he must do it for himself.

Drug abuse is a complex problem. As many as twelve million people in the United States are using drugs in improper ways. The majority of the drug abusers are between the ages of nine and twenty-five. No one is sure how to solve the problem. Maybe you can help!

DRUG GLOSSARY

Acid	LSD
Acid-head	Frequent user of LSD
Bag	Packet of drugs
Bang	Injection of drugs
Barbs	Barbiturates
Bennies	Benzedrine, an amphetamine
Bindle	Packet of narcotics
Blast	Strong effect from a drug
Blue angels	Amytal, a barbiturate
Blue velvet	Paregoric and Pyribenzamine
Bombita	Amphetamine injection, sometimes taken with heroin
Bread	Money
Busted	Arrested
Chipping	Taking narcotics occasionally
Coasting	Under the influence of drugs
Cokie	Cocaine addict
Cold turkey	Sudden withdrawal of narcotics
Coming down	Recovering from a trip

Connection	Drug supplier
Cop	To obtain heroin
Cop out	Quit; take off
Crash	The effects of stopping the use of amphetamines
Cut	Dilute drugs by adding milk sugar
Dealer	Drug supplier
Dirty	Possessing drugs; liable to arrest if searched
Dollies	Dolophine, also known as methadone
Downers	Sedatives, alcohol, tranquilizers, and narcotics
Dynamite	High-grade heroin
Fix	Injection of narcotics
Flash	The initial feeling after injecting
Floating	Under the influence of drugs
Freak-out	Bad experience
Fuzz	The police
Gage	Marijuana
Goof balls	Sleeping pills
Grass	Marijuana
H	Heroin
Hard narcotics	Opiates, such as heroin and morphine
Hash	Hashish
Hay	Marijuana
Hearts	Dexedrine tablets (from the shape)
High	Under the influence of drugs
Hooked	Addicted
Horse	Heroin
Hustle	Activities to obtain money to buy drugs
Joint	Marijuana cigarette
Jolly beans	Pep pills
Junkie	Narcotics addict
Kick the habit	Stop using narcotics
Layout	Equipment for injecting drug
Lemonade	Poor heroin
Mainline	Inject drugs into a vein
Maintaining	Keeping at a certain level of drug effect
Manicure	Remove seeds and stems from marijuana
Meth-head	Habitual user of methamphetamine
Narc	Narcotics detective
O.D.	Overdose of narcotics
On the nod	Sleepy from narcotics
Panic	Shortage of narcotics on the market

Pot	Marijuana
Pusher	Drug peddler
Quill	A matchbook cover for sniffing narcotics
Reefer	Marijuana cigarette
Re-entry	Return from a trip
Roach	Marijuana butt
Run	An amphetamine binge
Satch cotton	Cotton used to strain drugs before injection
Score	Make a purchase of drugs
Shooting gallery	Place where addicts inject
Skin popping	Injecting drugs under the skin
Smoke	Wood alcohol
Snorting	Inhaling drugs
Snow	Cocaine
Speed	Methamphetamine
Speedball	An injection of a stimulant (cocaine) and a depressant (heroin)
Stash	Supply of drugs in a secure place
Stoolie	Informer
Strung out	Addicted
Tracks	Scars along veins after many injections
Turned on	Under the influence of drugs
Uppers	Stimulants
Weed	Marijuana
Yellow jacket	Nembutal, a barbiturate
Yen sleep	A drowsy, restless state during the withdrawal period

INDEX

JOHN GABRIEL NAVARRA, the author of *Drugs and Man,* is director of environmental studies and experimental honors programs and was for ten years chairman of the division of science at Jersey City State College. As both teacher and writer, Dr. Navarra has an international reputation. He was the teacher of the first televised science course to be offered in the South when he was on the faculty of East Carolina University. He has written a number of trade books for young readers, adult science books, and college textbooks, and is the senior author of a complete series of science books, grades kindergarten through nine, that are used by millions of school children throughout the United States. At one time in his career Dr. Navarra served as a chemist in the Bureau of Chemistry of the New York Produce Exchange. He knows the chemistry of living systems through firsthand experience.

TOBY NAVARRA, the illustrator, is Dr. Navarra's daughter-in-law. She is married to John, Jr., who teaches at Seton Hall. Mrs. Navarra attended Upsala College and Jersey City State. She has taught second grade and presently devotes most of her time to her two children, Yolanda and John III. Mrs. Navarra has displayed her paintings and won awards at numerous art shows. She has taught art and beginning guitar in summer programs at Seton Hall.

COPY 1

613.8 Navarra, John
N Gabriel

Drugs and man

DATE			
1-17-80	fac	AP 21 '92	
2-1-80	FEB 2	MY 12 '92	
2-19-80	FEB 13		
2-27-80	FEB 23	JA 19 '94	
4-1-80	JAN 24 '85		
4-8-80	FEB 5 '85		
4-14-80	FEB 12 '85		
4/14/80	DEC 19 '86		
SEP 11	JAN 20 '87		
DEC 21	JAN 29 '87		
JAN 11	JAN 27 '86		
1-21-82	JA 29 '92		